TABLE OF CONTENTS

INTRODUCTION 5

OUR MESSAGE 9

OUR ASSETS 13

OUR CREATIVE 19

OUR SOCIAL MEDIA 25

AUDIENCE DEMOGRAPHICS AND REACH..31

NTRODUCTION

These guidelines were created to preserve and promote the future of YouthBuild Louisville.

As the organization grows and the workload increases, we are likely to encounter staff expansion, turnover, and outsourced labor.

In the face of inevitable change, it's important to solidify YouthBuild Louisville's visual representation so that our marketing efforts remain consistent, and therefore, recognizable in the community.

These guidelines outline how our creative materials should look and feel to ensure our legacy is accurately depicted for years to come.

OUR MISSION

YouthBuild Louisville champions young adults to be great citizens who build productive and sustainable communities.

USING THIS GUIDE

Having a consistent image is essential to telling our story and resonating with our audiences.

Our identity guidelines cover the basics of YouthBuild Louisville's visual elements and are

organized into five main sections:

1. OUR MESSAGE

2. OUR ASSETS

3. OUR CREATIVE

4. OUR SOCIAL MEDIA

5. AUDIENCE DEMOGRAPHICS AND REACH

While it is beneficial to familiarize yourself with the complete guide, we understand time is of the

essence. So jump in wherever it makes the most sense for you and the task at hand, **and reach out**

to Emily or Stacy if you run into any questions.

OUR MESSAGE

OUR MESSAGE: YOUTHBUILD IS BUILDING LIVES

YouthBuild Louisville's mission is to capitalize on the positive energy of young adults by helping

them rebuild their communities and their own lives with a commitment to work, education,

responsibility and family. YouthBuild aids unemployed and undereducated young people,

ages 16-24, in building affordable housing for homeless and low-income families in their own

communities. They split their time between vocational training and the classroom, where they

earn their GED or high school diploma, learn to be community leaders and prepare for jobs or

college.

OUR ASSETS

OUR LOGO

"For many, a logo is the brand. It is instantly recognisable, it is catchy in the same way a good song is, and it could be easily drawn."
Eleanor Ross

From tee shirts to stickers to profile pictures to banners, our logo is how we are identified in the community. It's important that our visual representation is consistent and easily recognizable, which means it should only be used with our primary colors.

1) [The Master Logo can be found here in PDF format.](#) This will generally suffice for most printing and publishing needs.

2) If you have a special request for a "Vector" file, [we have one in Illustrator (.ai) which can be located here](#). You will not be able to open this file if you don't have the program.

PROGRAM LOGOS, AFFILIATES, AND CO-BRANDING

Our Building Lives program has developed a unique logo to be use specifically for those events.

The Building Lives logo should be used in its native green and black colors. White on a solid color background is also acceptable.

In addition to our program-specific logos, we have affiliate logos to be used on co-branded events.

AmeriCorps and the Mayor's Summer Works programs are examples of affiliate logos that we often co-brand with our logo and events. You can download these logos, as well as specific sponsor logos, here. Ask Emily or Stacy if you need help!

CREATING A BUSINESS CARD

Vertical Standard Business Card

1. Log into vistaprint.com
   admin@yblky.org
   ybl4257
2. Go to My Account/ My Portfolio
3. Find the Artwork labeled "Copy to use for new cards"
4. Click "Save a Copy"
5. Name the copy with the New Name for the Cards
6. Find the newly named artwork in the list and click "Edit"
7. Click "My Computer" to browse for the new PDF of the new Artwork
8. Upload
9. The new artwork will show in the "Images" area
10. Drag the new artwork over to the design
11. Click "Replace Image."
12. Delete the old artwork

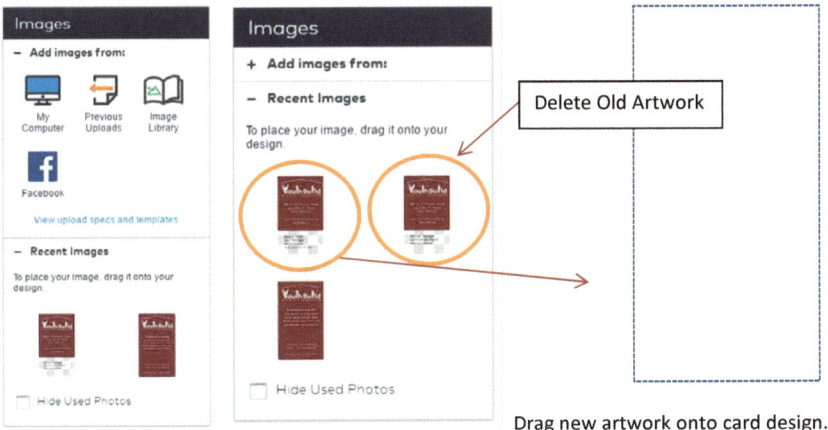

Drag new artwork onto card design.

13. Click "Next".
14. Review the design. If correct, [X] Check the "I have reviewed artwork…" box.
15. Select your quantity for the order – NEXT
16. [X] No Brilliant Finish (Included) – NEXT

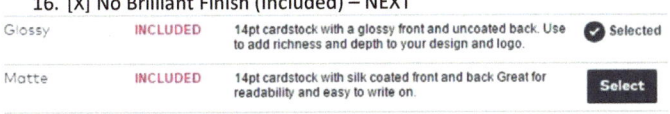

17. Change it from "Matte" to "Glossy" - NEXT
18. NEXT, Go to Cart. Checkout.

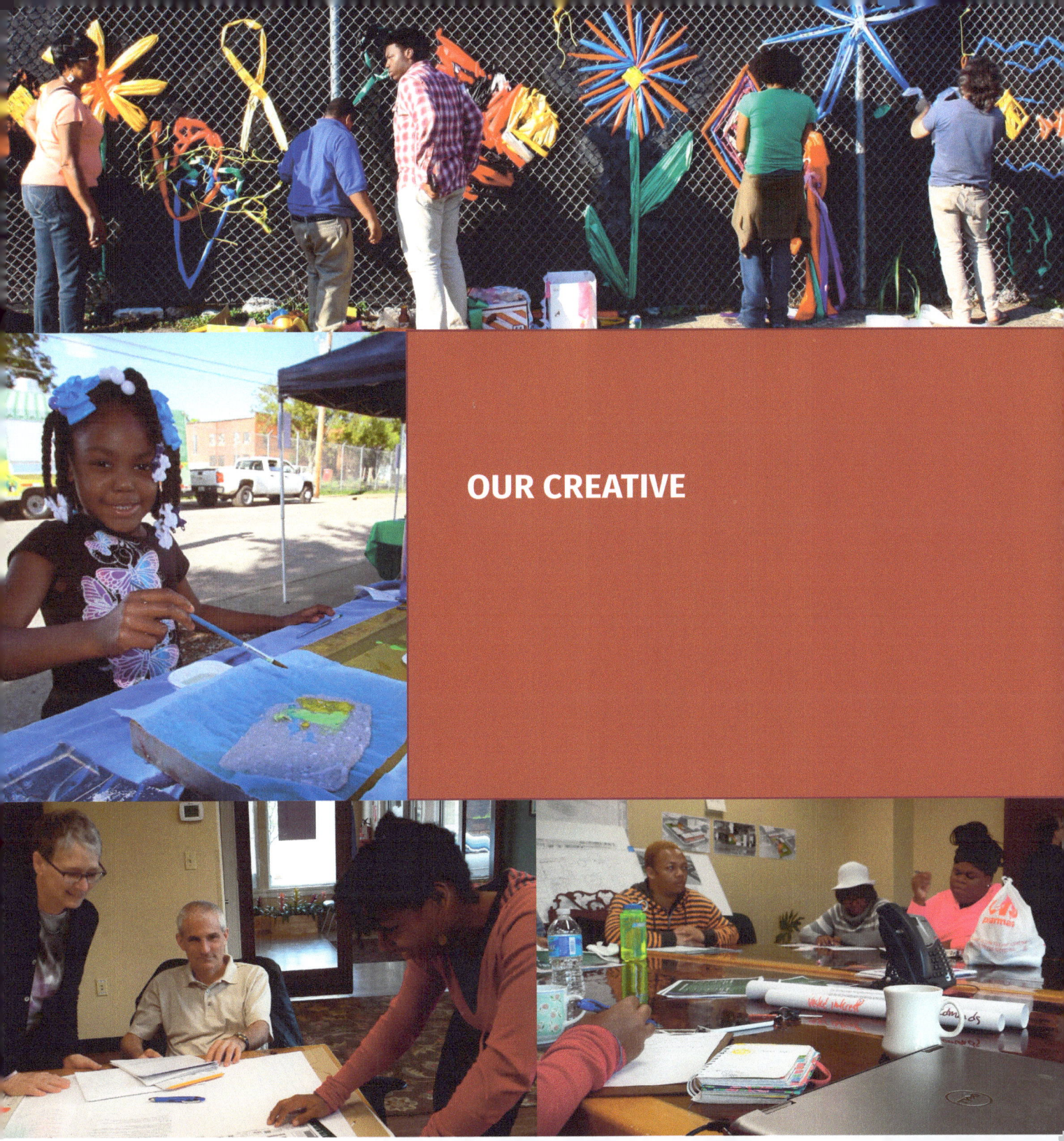

OUR CREATIVE

OUR COLOR PALETTE

R: 159 G: 33 B: 33
#9F2121
Pantone: 7627c

R: 0 G: 55 B: 100
#003764
Pantone: 648C

PRIMARY COLORS

R: 170 G: 123 B: 54
AA7B36
Pantone: 7558C

R: 98 G: 128 B: 159
#62809F
Pantone: 5415C

R: 80 G: 19 B: 18
#501312
Pantone: 4975C

R: 0 G: 104 B: 56
#006838
Pantone: 349C

SECONDARY COLORS

OUR FONTS

Museo Slab

Museo Slab should be used sparingly for callouts or informational details

Fira Sans

Fira Regular should be used for body text
Fira Bold should be used for headers

FFF_TUSJ

FFF_TUSJ should be used for headlines & titles

Fauna One

Fauna One can be used for body text and for headers

Click here to download the YouthBuild Fonts! One you have the fonts downloaded onto your

computer, simply right-click on the file and select "Install" to install the fonts onto your computer.

Once they are installed, you will be able to use them within all programs including Microsoft Word,

Microsoft Publisher, Microsoft PowerPoint, Adobe Illustrator, Adobe InDesign, etc.

CREATIVE EXAMPLES

WAYS TO GET INVOLVED

YouthBuild Louisville

AN EDUCATIONAL, TRAINING LIFE SKILLS & LEADERSHIP PROGRAM

VOLUNTEER
Put your talent, skills, and passion for service by participating as a volunteer with YouthBuild Louisville! You can experience the personal and professional benefits of channeling your energy to help improve the lives of people in your community!

MATERIAL DONATIONS
Visit us online at YBLKY.ORG to see the current Wish List of needed items. Big or small, all donations are appreciated!

MONITARY DONATIONS
A gift of cash or by credit card is the most straightforward way to support our work and the young people who are rebuilding their communities and their lives. As a 501(c)(3) organization, all donations are tax-deductible. Online donations are possible on our website.

SMOKETOWN CAMPUS

With broad community support and hands-on hard work, YouthBuild Louisville transformed a vacant urban commercial space into an oasis of beauty and thoughtfully integrated learning spaces in the heart of Smoketown. YBL consolidated 8 parcels of land in the Smoketown neighborhood. YouthBuild develops and provides essential programs and services for young people concurrent with the evolving landscape of our campus and community. This thriving corner of Smoketown is an anchor and essential for the wellbeing of the youth we serve and the growing economic health of the neighborhood.

LEARN MORE ONLINE
- yblky.org
- /youthbuild
- YouthBuild Louisville
- youthbuild_louisville
- info@yblky.org

BUILDING HOMES & CHANGING FUTURES

800 S. Preston Street • Louisville, KY 40203
(502) 290-6121 • yblky.org

Click here for a link to the General Information Brochure template

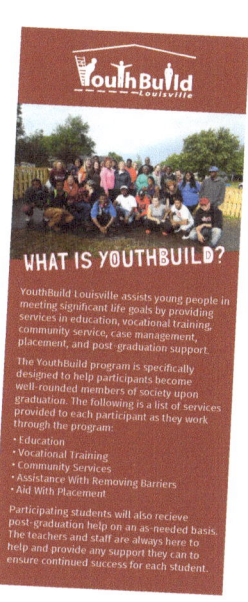

WHAT IS YOUTHBUILD?

YouthBuild Louisville assists young people in meeting significant life goals by providing services in education, vocational training, community service, case management, placement, and post-graduation support.

The YouthBuild program is specifically designed to help participants become well-rounded members of society upon graduation. The following is a list of services provided to each participant as they work through the program:

- Education
- Vocational Training
- Community Services
- Assistance With Removing Barriers
- Aid With Placement

Participating students will also recieve post-graduation help on an as-needed basis. The teachers and staff are always here to help and provide any support they can to ensure continued success for each student.

Click here for a link to the
Get Involved Rack Card template

CONSTRUCTION

PRE-NURSING (CNA)

NOW ENROLLING!
AN EDUCATIONAL, TRAINING LIFE SKILLS & LEADERSHIP PROGRAM

Applications Due: 7/31/18 | Orientation Starts: 8/2018

BENEFITS
- Weekly living allowance (Approximately $100 per week, based on 100% attendance and participation)
- Potential of 4 College Credits at end of program
- Savings Plan (Up to $50 per month, based on 100% attendance and participation)
- College prep and tutoring
- Assistance with college entry paperwork
- College Scholarships available thru AmeriCorps Award
- Leadership and life skills training
- Work experience / Resume writing
- Remove barriers to success
- Community & Social networking

Your Course. Your Choice.
- /youthbuild
- YouthBuild Louisville
- youthbuild_lousiville
- info@yblky.org

REQUIREMENTS
- Be between ages of 18-24
- Be able to complete an intense two week orientation (Unpaid)
- Make a 1 year commitment to CHANGE!
- Be available Mon-Fri from 8:30am-4:00pm
- Be willing to work toward education goals (GED/College & Vocational)
- Willing to work in a TEAM setting to accomplish goals
- Willing to work on construction & environmental projects
- Commit to hard work and full participation
- Be self-motivated & self-disciplined
- Be drug-free
- Willing to participate

YouthBuild Louisville champions young adults to be great citizens who build productive lives and sustainable communities.

OPPORTUNITIES

CONSTRUCTION
Students earn a Pre-Apprenticeship in construction, First Aid, CPR, and OSHA Certifications. Community projects and specialized training. Hourly wage possible once on-site. Assistance with job placement.

PRE-NURSING (CNA)
Enrollment in Certified Nursing or Medical Nursing program. Ongoing support in pre-nursing education and placement in local medical field. Work with our partners, acting as community educator.

ENVIRONMENTAL/ LANDSCAPING
Earn certification in Horticulture and basic environmental education. Opportunities for certifications in arboriculture, agriculture and watershed study. Assistance with job placement.

CULINARY
Exposed to all facets of restaurant activities including serving, hostessing, ordering, kitchen prep and general administration. ServSafe Certification. Assistance with job placement.

Must have GED/HS Diploma

YouthBuild Louisville
800 S. Preston Street
Louisville, KY 40203
(502) 290-6121

REQUEST AN APPLICATION BE EMAILED TO YOU@WWW.YBLKY.ORG OR COME TO 800 S. PRESTON & FILL OUT AN APPLICATION (Bring Two Forms of ID)

CALL (502) 290-6121 FOR MORE INFORMATION

Click here for a link to the New Student Registration template

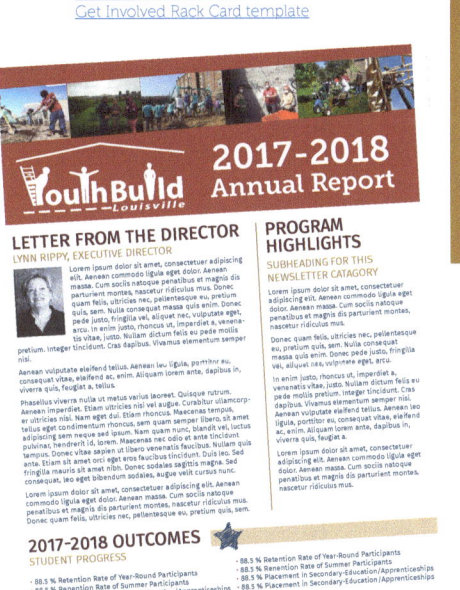

YouthBuild Louisville

2017-2018 Annual Report

LETTER FROM THE DIRECTOR
LYNN RIPPY, EXECUTIVE DIRECTOR

Lorem ipsum dolor sit amet, consectetuer adipiscing elit. Aenean commodo ligula eget dolor. Aenean massa. Cum sociis natoque penatibus et magnis dis parturient montes, nascetur ridiculus mus. Donec quam felis, ultricies nec, pellentesque eu, pretium quis, sem. Nulla consequat massa quis enim. Donec pede justo, fringilla vel, aliquet nec, vulputate eget, arcu. In enim justo, rhoncus ut, imperdiet a, venenatis vitae, justo. Nullam dictum felis eu pede mollis pretium. Integer tincidunt. Cras dapibus. Vivamus elementum semper nisi.

Aenean vulputate eleifend tellus. Aenean leo ligula, porttitor eu, consequat vitae, eleifend ac, enim. Aliquam lorem ante, dapibus in, viverra quis, feugiat a, tellus.

Phasellus viverra nulla ut metus varius laoreet. Quisque rutrum. Aenean imperdiet. Etiam ultricies nisi vel augue. Curabitur ullamcorper ultricies nisi. Nam eget dui. Etiam rhoncus. Maecenas tempus, tellus eget condimentum rhoncus, sem quam semper libero, sit amet adipiscing sem neque sed ipsum. Nam quam nunc, blandit vel, luctus pulvinar, hendrerit id, lorem. Maecenas nec odio et ante tincidunt tempus. Donec vitae sapien ut libero venenatis faucibus. Nullam quis ante. Etiam sit amet orci eget eros faucibus tincidunt. Duis leo. Sed fringilla mauris sit amet nibh. Donec sodales sagittis magna. Sed consequat, leo eget bibendum sodales, augue velit cursus nunc.

Lorem ipsum dolor sit amet, consectetuer adipiscing elit. Aenean commodo ligula eget dolor. Aenean massa. Cum sociis natoque penatibus et magnis dis parturient montes, nascetur ridiculus mus. Donec quam felis, ultricies nec, pellentesque eu, pretium quis, sem.

PROGRAM HIGHLIGHTS

SUBHEADING FOR THIS NEWSLETTER CATAGORY

Lorem ipsum dolor sit amet, consectetuer adipiscing elit. Aenean commodo ligula eget dolor. Aenean massa. Cum sociis natoque penatibus et magnis dis parturient montes, nascetur ridiculus mus.

Donec quam felis, ultricies nec, pellentesque eu, pretium quis, sem. Nulla consequat massa quis enim. Donec pede justo, fringilla vel, aliquet nec, vulputate eget, arcu.

In enim justo, rhoncus ut, imperdiet a, venenatis vitae, justo. Nullam dictum felis eu pede mollis pretium. Integer tincidunt. Cras dapibus. Vivamus elementum semper nisi. Aenean vulputate eleifend tellus. Aenean leo ligula, porttitor eu, consequat vitae, eleifend ac, enim. Aliquam lorem ante, dapibus in, viverra quis, feugiat a.

Lorem ipsum dolor sit amet, consectetuer adipiscing elit. Aenean commodo ligula eget dolor. Aenean massa. Cum sociis natoque penatibus et magnis dis parturient montes, nascetur ridiculus mus.

2017-2018 OUTCOMES
STUDENT PROGRESS

- 88.3 % Retention Rate of Year-Round Participants
- 88.3 % Retention Rate of Summer Participants
- 88.3 % Placement in Secondary-Education/Apprenticeships
- 88.3 % Retention Rate of Year-Round Participants
- 88.3 % Retention Rate of Summer Participants
- 88.3 % Placement in Secondary-Education/Apprenticeships

Click here for a link to the Annual Report template

YouthBuild Louisville

NEW OPPORTUNITIES

ENVIRONMENTAL/ LANDSCAPING*
Earn certification in Horticulture and basic environmental education. Opportunities for certifications in arboriculture, agriculture and watershed study. Assistance with job placement.

CULINARY*
Exposed to all facets of restaurant activities including serving, hostessing, ordering, kitchen prep and general administration. ServSafe Certification. Assistance with job placement.

INTERNATIONAL TRAVEL INTERNSHIPS
New opportunities arise each year for students to travel abroad. The aim of these international collaborations is to learn to transform fallow urban land into a productive and engaging greenspace fueling local entrepreneurship through the training and employment of local youth.

* Must have GED or HS Diploma

Click here for a link to the
New Student Rack Cards
template

OUR SOCIAL MEDIA

SOCIAL MEDIA POSTS

Social media posts should contain the following elements in order to maximize exposure and provide a

cohesive look within all platforms:

1. Brief description and purpose of the events

2. Hashtag: #youthbuildlouisville

3. Picture or video

4. Tags of people and organizations represented in the post

5. Mark location

SOCIAL MEDIA EXAMPLES - FACEBOOK

YouthBuild Louisville is with Liz Scarfpin Weiss and 6 others
February 2 at 4:33pm

National Wear Red Day - support American Heart ❤ Month by wearing red and increase awareness surrounding heart disease. About 80% of cardiac events can be prevented with education and lifestyle changes. Thank you Norton Healthcare for supporting Go Red for Women! **#youthbuildlouisville**

👍 Like   💬 Comment   ↪ Share

😊❤ 17   Top Comments ▾

YouthBuild Louisville
February 3 at 12:00pm

ECHO program provides new experiences for YBL students! Check out ED Lynn Rippy at this week's press conference regarding this recent grant. **#youthbuildlouisville**
http://ow.ly/o2cd30iafYN

Youth program ran by Metro Parks Department receives grant
The West Louisville Outdoor Recreation Initiative engages nearly 1,000 young people in after-school programs geared toward nature.
WLKY.COM

 Like    Comment   Share

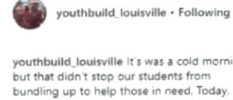

youthbuild_louisville · Following

youthbuild_louisville It's was a cold morning but that didn't stop our students from bundling up to help those in need. Today, students volunteered at @francis_kitchen for their Friday service project. We love our community so we give back! #gettingthingsdone #americorps #smoketown #louisvilleky #louisvilleigers #louisvillekentucky #nonprofit #youthbuild **#youthbuildlouisville**

50 likes

FEBRUARY 2

Add a comment...   ···

SOCIAL MEDIA EXAMPLES - TWITTER

 YouthBuildLouisville @youthbuildlouky · 7 Nov 2017
Join us for lunch November 15th from 12-1 pm and learn more about
@youthbuildlouky #youthbuildlouisville
Contact Development@YBLKY.org to reserve your FREE seat!

◯   ⭤ 1   ♡ 3

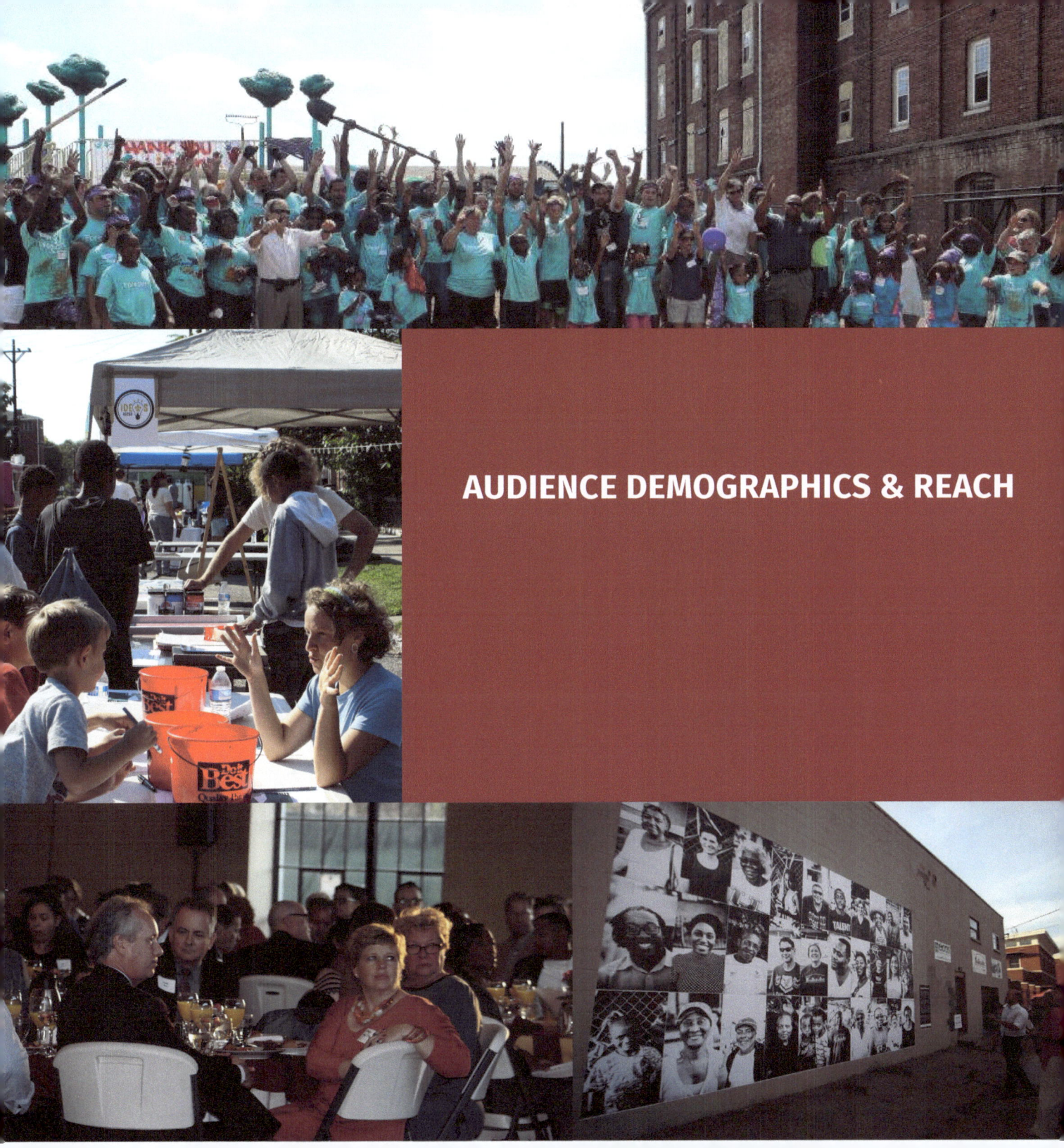

AUDIENCE DEMOGRAPHICS & REACH

OCIAL MEDIA DEMOGRAPHIC AUDIENCE ANALYSIS

GENDER

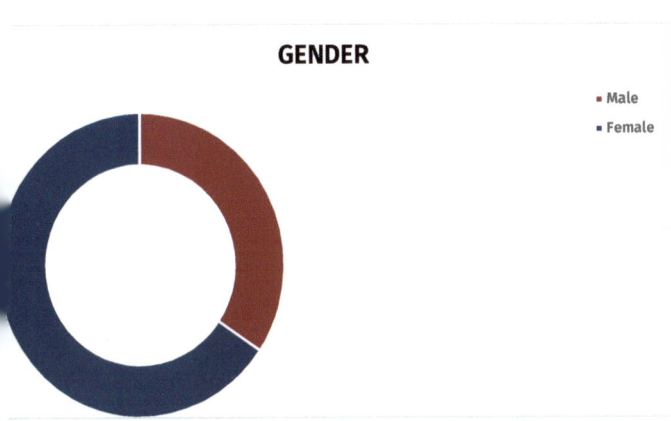

- Male
- Female

AGE

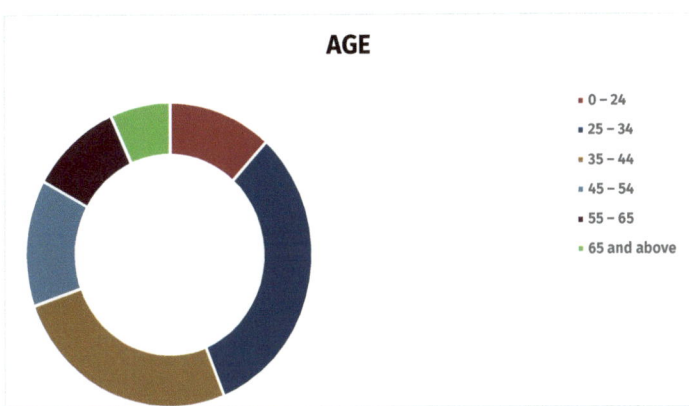

- 0 – 24
- 25 – 34
- 35 – 44
- 45 – 54
- 55 – 65
- 65 and above

INCOME

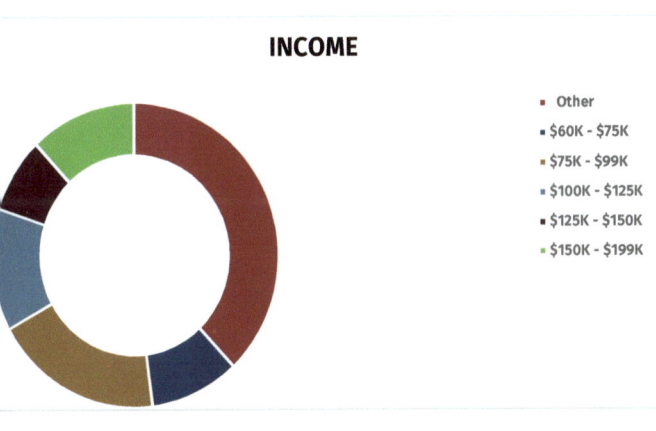

- Other
- $60K - $75K
- $75K - $99K
- $100K - $125K
- $125K - $150K
- $150K - $199K

PROFESSION

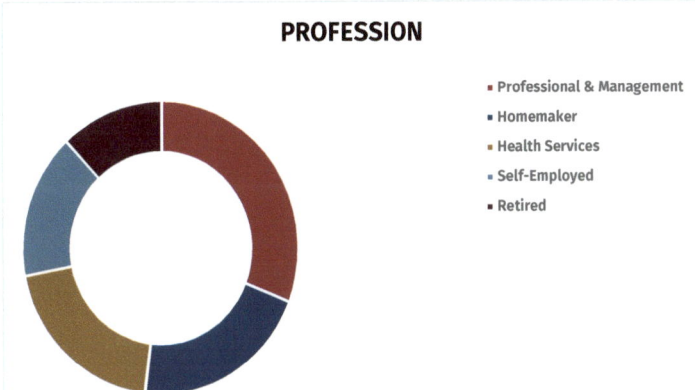

- Professional & Management
- Homemaker
- Health Services
- Self-Employed
- Retired

SUGGESTED TARGET AUDIENCE & REACH

Based on social media data, our target audience should be young professionals in Louisville, between the age of 25 and 44, who work 9-to-5 jobs, with interests in politics, current events, business, and news.

Suggested Donation Channels Other Than Current Fundraising Events

1. Large corporation with social responsibilities focusing on education

    a. [Top giving foundations in Kentucky](#)

    b. [Corporate giving programs in Kentucky](#)

2. Companies with matching gift programs

    a. [List of Louisville companies with matching gift programs](#)

3. Sponsor a student (mentor/mentee) program with leaders from different companies

4. Events targeting the demographic, such as painting events, local art auction, etc.

www.ingramcontent.com/pod-product-compliance
Lightning Source LLC
Chambersburg PA
CBHW041533280526
45792CB00004B/1483